dormilona

Connie Mae Oliver

BURROW PRESS | ORLANDO, FL

The poet is donating author royalties earned from this book to the Middle East Children's Alliance, for more information visit mecaforpeace.org.

© Connie Mae Oliver, 2025
Cover photo: courtesy of the author
Book design: Ryan Rivas
ISBN: 978-1-941681-34-3
Library of Congress Control Number: 2024947472
Published by Burrow Press.
First edition. First printing.
Special thanks to the Sullivan Creative Writing Program for support in producing this book.

Para mi mamá y mi abuela, Manola y Gladys

contents

light sleep 6

RORAIMA 22

azabache 42

deep sleep 54

sleep data 66

light sleep

...y en la orilla del silencio
se le añudará el tañío
cuando yo mande a parar
el trueno y el desafío.

El trueno y el desafío

Your thoughts go down the waterway
away from you who pursues them.

The moon landing
it lands in your heart
creating more land
more than there had been
until this hour.

Mareada

Te vas sola
al Parque Central. Buscando desmayarte, ahí
entre los árboles ingleses y las piedras
por alguna razón que ni tú
entiendes bien.

Deep sleep dwells in the bar of light that crayons the wall
and makes waves of anything.

I am mapping the activity in my brain, chasing synapses maybe. Like passing my hand over a flame to understand a volcano.

Sometimes my mother and I discuss what it feels like to be lost in a forest. She says my grandmother is the forest she is lost in. She says she is sorry for having placed me in a forest of my own, she is sorry that I haven't found my way out. We wander in our respective forests.

I google near-death experiences, prone to believe the ones that describe it as routine. Like falling asleep.

When I drive I think about the passage of time. I think lots about how something won't happen for a long while, and then there it is happening. The temporal distance turns out to be no distance at all; the wait, no matter how long, is always nothing. Time the mother, time the story, time the amniotic vertigo.

When I started writing this book it was different. But as writing went on, and as pages were added, death was brushed in. I rolled Gladys' hair in melon-colored velcro curlers in 1998, I wrote this book, she died. I started the car, drove, then arrived. Just as "empty space" is a contradiction, so too is the alleged space between temporal markers.

One can be as alive as dead. But what a heavy word, "dead." Not especially better, but different, is "muerta." Perhaps it's worse; a troubling evocation of "morder" and a grim little rhyme with "puerta."

Isla Margarita is twenty-five miles north of the Venezuelan mainland, in the South Caribbean. My family took a ferry there from Puerto La Cruz. I had just read Island of the Blue Dolphins for my fifth-grade English class, and this coincided with my first dolphin sighting; they chased us all the way there.

My grandmother was fine. We talked about how at eighty-seven she was this and that and irascible but endearingly, alive though in a garbled way. She was mean, but in a manner we all learned to flatten into character. Then one day she fell, and then I don't know. The day came back to me, in 2001, at the front gate of her house, when I said goodbye and brushed the intrusive thoughts about never seeing her again, because the government was getting stricter, because whatever, because because.

It isn't that I don't understand how things work. How an eighty-seven year old woman falls and something breaks, unlocking death, which was formerly kept aside like a rolled up rug or a plastic covered chair.

It's that we couldn't see her. We couldn't sit in the Valencia heat, swatting mosquitoes, hearing ice cream bells in the distance, wearing white, gazing at the mountains.

Bueno. En fin, I signed up for neurofeedback sessions with Behavioral Associates. They shipped a device, instructing me to fasten it to the parietal ridge of my head and connect it wirelessly to my phone. "Mindlyft" was the name for the training sessions meant to condition the brain to adapt to specific neurowave presets. Bound to this wiring I fell into sleep. My programming was set to increase beta waves and decrease thetas. Or maybe it was the other way around.

I tried talking to Gladys over the phone but she didn't completely know it was me. I felt that she knew it was me in her peripheral dreams, but she never said my name, she echoed what the neighbor told her to say, she hummed.

I crouched in front of someone's house on Ditmars Avenue, listening to her chirruping voice in Valencia; the phone a periscope with a foggy viewfinder. Just as I was nearly finished writing, she vanished, taking her things with her.

Look at how the moon faces us, shines on us, quieter than the sun.

We don't even know how the moon happened (do we?) We don't know if it was once part of Earth, or if it fell into our arms.

Manzanilla

Quita todo, con la fuerza de mi voluntad
el espíritu santo te esponja la almohada. A ver—
a pues
así no
no le eches hielo
por haber comido azúcar
por haberle echado
azúcar a las caraotas. Como se las comen
en el estado Sucre, de donde viene la mata
y la insomnia, se te hinchan los pies y así no puedes
pero yo te cargo
te camino los zapatos
no me canso
ni me duermo
te pido que me dibujes
una cabrita – Así no, así no,
Al fin me dibujas una cajita
y me dices Pues adentro está
dormida.

Light sleep

Rolling eyes
in departures
in Maiquetía Airport
several soldiers
view me from above and say
¿Te has desmayado? rifles slung
like messenger bags
¿Te has desmayado? Mírale le cara.
Eyes rolling back
Los pajaritos me hacen las clinejas y me cantan.

A los dieciséis
me perdí en el aeropuerto
suelta en
un sueño
tetracromático y polvoroso
todas las veces que paramos ahí
a despedirnos
de los abuelos
las primas
los tíos
hasta los soldados.

¡Ceniciéntate!
Más pálida que una hoja,
lo que te quedan son
los lunares.
The moon lands in me.

The soldiers help me off
the military cot
so that I can fly back.

Before coming to I hear
Gladys in the future
as she passes her deceased brother's house:
"Ahí vivía mi hermano."

El piloto perdido

The printout at Mt. Sinai
says "Syncope" and "Patient
can only strum in a triplet rhythm."

I took the 7 nowhere
and watched the airplanes coasting.

I am afraid of flying and I do it and do it.

It's the same lifted air that sends my eyes rolling back
that drops my sister
down the spiral staircase
that throws my father from the ladder
my brother sees blood and falls forward.

Poor decisions by upper mgmt
make us cats in a picture book trapped up top
suspended
super kiu &reaching down
with our paws to be saved.

A head rush placed my other selves in that world
and placed me in this and here it was slumber
that placed those worlds in us.

Hypnagogia

I never know I've slept.

Back at the airport is the saddest dream the only living dream I know
in the lil tiny room
in Concourse B
when MIA used to allow smoking.

Y pues ahora
the meniscus farther
above water space
a line retreating
in the gold-threaded
terminal in the morning
a delayed return.

La vuelta

I will go to sleep once
my hair is wrapped
with the pterodactyl clips.

We're going
to the center of Valencia
to take my passport photos
this is why my hair
will be straight tomorrow.

Gladys is in her dormilona
in the kitchen
pouring whiskey
she tells me *Go back*
but I say *No.*

When she visited us in Miami she said
Have you ever dialed 911?

Dial it she said

so you can practice & know how to.

Do you mean right now?
She was like *Anda.*

Well, I don't
have an emergency
she was like

Say wrong number, it's just for practice.

911 what is your emergency?
Nothing I said.
No darkness in the dark darkened still and floral.

I did not forget
who I was last time I passed out
I had instead
never known and that was
the worst.

My grandmother I have said is "the worst"
because of her sharp manicure
the mean songs she sings
she gave me the middle finger
when I was eight and I remember thinking
whatever.

She wrote poems
they're trapped in Valencia
in a cabinet with Avon samples.

I said to her I would translate them
but I've left her at the edge of oblivion
with no one like me there to not
take it from her
to not wring my hands.

Driving alone in Miami
after a day in the A/C
the steering wheel burns.
I pass the airport and resent her in a loved state
only the eldest granddaughter knows.
You can't talk to me that way.
You can't talk to her that way.

I tried to take a picture of the moon
but it looked like a speck
impossible & I guess
it's true you can't photograph her
she's the only one
haunting her own house
filling it up with the bitterest
and as it turns out truest
night song.

When you are outside you are asleep

A humid trek sends me up an unpaved downhill
street in Naguanagua
to return the empty Chinotto
liters and bring full
ones back for us to eat the cassava
and the tray of Guayanés cheese
a tía brought to the house and is upset
about having gone unthanked.

Impossible to rest
in the favorite spaces
designated as they are
full of combs and balms
and coins and low frequency
and higher frequency lowered.

RORAIMA

*¿Con qué se seca la cara
el que no carga pañuelo?
¿Pá'que se limpia las patas
el que va a dormir en el suelo?*

El que va a dormir en el suelo

Me cuentan:

Ingenieros de los Estados Unidos
                    les decían a los obreros en Zulia:

GET YOUR MAC & DALES

to start working the rigs

    Get your gear
    became
    Agarra tus Macundales

An entire syncretic etymology passed through

unannounced letters

Spanish submerged
and pulled
from
    the water
            rainbowed in oil
                ancient chroma
                      recent migrations

words folded
and then

      opened into
      longer ones
            extra u's and i's and b's

That's not how you say BANANA Carolina Jose Andreina tells me
    as if to ask,
        Who threw all that sugar into your Castellano?
        Who pulled all the pink pearls from your water?

In the land of poets I went looking for music, looked
in their cupboards and under
        their fleur-de-lys couch cushions
        pero na'! Na guará! Lástima
        nunca salió tu gusano de seda ni se convirtió
        en linda mariposa.

Corotos

Cepipeine, Trucutu, taza,
gorro, periódico, otro cepillo
pero de dientes, dientes
zapatos de goma, caracol
de no sé dónde, de Los Roques
cien Bolívares; una moneda
sobre, caja de sobres, varios sombreros enfatizados
porta retrato sin retrato
foto sin porta retrato
sin cabezas, sólo manos con copas.

Copas, cinco—se te rompió una
medio paquete de
Harina Pan,
libro con disco—Píter Pan
otro libro—Murder Chi Wrote by La Gata Triste.

El balcón sobre mirando Valencia
verdecita y rosadita
paliza si me acerco demasiado.

El inalámbrico, el cofre de
España, las tortuguitas de vidrio
el nacimiento hasta febrero
los discos del tío (Supertrán)
las matas de adentro, las matas de afuera
las sillas blancas de hierro que se mecen

y me pellizcan las piernas.

Frascos de aspirina con pastillas diferentes, Lexotanil
licuadora, corbata de nadie, VE ACHE ESE (un teipe)
de Back to the Future parte dos.

Gladys
sé que sabes que te buscan
sé que quieres que te encuentren.

Catires

When Por Estas Calles
came on Gladys told us
to either shut up or go away.
¡Chito!

My tooth fell out
while I detangled
Machi's hair.
Chinotto went up
my nose when
Miguel imitated Gladys

pretended his Frescolita was whiskey
and over-enunciated the consonants.
She came out and pinched him
we retreated into the green kitchen
chomping on Club Sociales.

We climbed into tío Enriquito's Bronco
where we found him on a clandestine call—
1,000 Bolívares for each of us
if we moved along.

On the floor of concourse E
we kids play Stratego until they call our rows
Mamá y Papá cross their arms and turn to gaze out the airport windows.

Later I touch Mamá's hand on the 12A armrest
and she says *Don't forget to look at the mountains*
you got the window seat so you could.

They form tiny moving daguerreotypes
café con café
I think of those Andes mint chocolates at Navarro—
how we never buy them but seem always to have them
how we used to live in their snowy middle.

¿Cuántas botellas me trajiste?
Dos nomás
¿Y cuantas te quieres llevar?
Una nomás
¿Te importa si lleno la Fanta con Coca Cola?
Sí, o sea; no, está bien, gracias.

Hallaca

Ingredientes:

carne   yuca rallada
tierra
fruta
azabache
trigo

Preparación de la masa

                     En una olla
                     mezcla la harina
                     con agua, sal, y algo más

                     Recuerda que
                     pasan las décadas y cada año
                     trabajan menos
                     estos chamos, FLOJOS,
                     que no entienden lo que es
                     darle
                     metal contra metal

En Panamá nos llevaron a la compañía
y nos dieron bolsas
enormes, ballenitas de plástico. Llénenlas con
lo que quieran
compliments of Savoy Brands.

Empresas Polar

With our combined wares
we went to live for a month
in Carora; a once remote town on the
Morere River, a region
called Altagracia, where French
oenologists told la doña
she could cultivate wine
in her subtropical country.

Mamá let us make bags and bags and bags
of microwave popcorn
she took us to the main road where
a woman straightened my hair and gave me Bubbaloo
pink with a liquid center.

Papá kept the books for Bodegas Pomar—
We are making good wine in our own country.

These are our vineyards
our tributary full of deadly whirlpools
our wine siphoned from river water.

That ancient fluid under
now the bodies of dissenters under
and before that other dissenters under others.

We make our own wine
our food and our fossils yield the mal ojo
from up where—they come
they go—nobody
left nobody drinks
not wine anyway
not ours.

Gladys received us
back in Valencia with a pitcher of papaya juice
and a scowl augmented
by her gradient sunglasses.

I forget what she named her house
if it wasn't Andalucía it was something
in cursive copper. Between the gate
and the front door she kept a cluster
of deadly roses & was like *Anda
tócalas pa que veas.*

This is the last place I saw my grandfather
combing his hair with un cepipeine:

Please never grow up
to be someone who
seriously argues
about which version
of tyranny is best.

Chewing Bubbaloo all summer
sugar high, sugar that disintegrates your feet and pulls you under.

I washed my sister's hair and laid out the white dress
with flowers stitched invisibly in.

This is our wine it comes from heat
it ferments inside of toucan bellies
this is our beverage it is petro-pink and
made of Araguaney leaves.
This is our food that we mash and turn
in the stoneware. We call our past
but we call it wrong—this is all those
centuries rolled in—Mamá buys the Pillsbury
tube at Publix to make it.

Before we left Carora
vineyard employees were invited to see the first harvest
from a tethered hot air balloon.

>The children were not allowed
>but I can still visualize my forebears
>smiling in large sunglasses
>waving from above
>smaller in the sky but not diminishing
>not flying but
>aloft in their way.

Energía natural y full sabor

El mantel lo hizo tu tía Mercedes
la que jamás recuerdas
la que se acuerda siempre de ti.
My relative is stationary in the mind
remote and seated on a glass turtle in the cabinet,
bisabuela Conchita crocheting the first dress I ever wore.

A kitchen sequestering
tripping about the wall tiles
and their fleur-de-lys
lacquered in blue—lapicito azul
there in the distance
a relative knitting or chewing
leaving the wooden radio on high
to make people think we're home.

Enrique combed his fine hair down and the bell rang
he said it sounded like CLIN-tón!

The Jehovah's Witnesses came for his coffee splashed with brandy
the ice cream man came too
a Jesuit boy with a tiny white face
asked out his daughter,
to all of this he said Sure.

*At the Ignatius school they ran
asceticism drills,* Papá says, *You couldn't
begin to know what it was like.*
But what wouldn't I trade for a fast right now? Mainly
this bowl of tripe soup?
Slouching in the floral plastic chair I gesture
languid summer courses through my arm and
pops at the wrist.
*Don't be like that. Your grandmother made it.
Déjate de jueguitos que se enfría.*

Coromoto

Tío Marialionza
escribe por WhatsApp
que abrió un
negocio nuevo.

These messages
are transported
via the pipelines
of mad-mute circuitry.

- This service is needed
- People now lack the means
- The other business is but a gray family heirloom; a telescope
	pointing back to a time of blindness in brilliant coastal
	whitecaps at midday

Los tíos used
to work in a shop &
we used to organize their oaky
cologney chiffoniers.

The sun keeps collecting
its due keeps siphoning.

Gladys in a split phone screen
asks who is speaking
and who am I and *Oh
it's you.*

*One day I will translate
your poems*, I say,
if you want.

I know my uncle has started
a coffin-making business
to carry the weight. It enters a ground
formerly emptied
now the porous earth takes back
something.

A life of pulling and plunging
in the hydraulic turn
the Hydra replacing
each vanquished woe—
¿Abuela? ¿Aló?

El Tao del Taller

Tío Marialionza
nos trae Chis Tris
y así pasamos el tiempo:
chewing.

In the upstairs office of
Hidralcar—Hidráulicos Carabobo
there is a Gateway computer
with a banner-making program. We make
so many on the invoice printer.

- Fabricar la factura
- Oler a gasolina
- Construir grúas
- Tener un pen pal en Francia, los papelitos vienen de tan lejos

A certain industrial blue
is splashed on the walls of a workplace.
I watch my uncles in construction belts
the silver hammers slung
from their jacket loops.

Gladys in bifocals
at the desk
telling me I look stupid
when I give myself
Chiclet teeth—

You could inherit this company
if you want, and do you even know what we do? What a crane is?
Your uncle, who left school in the 7th grade
builds them, builds engines and what else.
And you, who are you even writing to?

Noviembre 1999

Señorita Connie Mei Concepción,

    Querida niña linda, te amo con amor de abuela y de madre, ya que tú eres mi primera nieta, mi "cuchinaza" como te llamaba cuando eras pequeña, sé que no suena muy bonito, pero qué le vamos a hacer si yo soy medio loca ya que invento cada cosa, pero es con mucho cariño que te llamaba así. Hoy eres mi orgullo y satisfacción, junto a tus hermanitos. Eres aparte de bella, inteligente, lista y de gran corazón. Querida mía dentro de poco vas a cumplir tus primeros quince y no sabes cuanto deseo estar junto a ti en un momento de gran significado para ti y todos tus familiares y amigos.

La circunstancia no ha _____ _____ porque eso sucede y la verdad que lo lamento mucho, pero mi corazón y pensamientos están contigo y con todos ustedes en tu memorable fecha. Recibe todo mi amor, y de
tus abuelitos, tías, primos y demás, recibe muchos besos y sobre todo concéntrate ese día para que sientas el calor de nuestros brazos que te rodean y

Cuchinaza, June 2019

     ¡Dile que estás bien!
      Dile que estoy bien
       aquí también tienes tus primas y
a tu amiga.

     ¡No te rías! Dile 'sí, a veces
     escribo.'

     Dile gracias.
       Gracias.

     Dile, 'Connie, te quiero.'
       Okei.

¡Dile!
     Espera, que está buscando una foto de su mamá ...

     ¡Dile! Gladys, dile.
Dile, Gladys; 'Yo te quiero mucho.'
Anda—

tírale un beso.

Dile que la quieres mucho. Dile: ¡Figúrate!
   Bueno.

{Abuela, te quiero muchísimo, y sé que tú me quieres también} Ah ah,
a-ha Connie—co co co co...
las circunstancias que te rodean.

azabache

*En la soledad profunda
el pecho del medanal,
el romance que lo arrulla—
¿Qué culpa tengo señores
si me encuentra el que me busca?*

Si me encuentra el que me busca

Cuando dice "la porfía" es así como el encuentro entre el diablo y Florentino. Cuando habla de "noche de fiero chubasco" es decir que está lloviendo bastante; un chubasco de lluvia. En la "enlutada llanura" es algo muy solo, pues, misterioso. "Encendidas chipolas"; chipolas son lámparas de kerosene, como algo que alumbra. Y a su vez, es un golpe de Joropo que se llama "chipola" que es un ritmo de esos que estoy diciendo son como fuertes; con carácter. Cuando dice que en el rancho del peón alumbran, bueno, es donde vive el que trabaja en el llano, en la casa ahí. Cuando dice que "adentro suena el capacho," el capacho es el 'capacho' de la maraca, de lo que está compuesta la maraca, las semillas que lleva adentro. Y bueno lo de que afuera bate la lluvia, pues que la lluvia se escucha afuera. "Vena en corazón de cedro," es como el corazón del árbol, pues, las venas que lleva el árbol por dentro, el árbol de cedro, y cuando habla del "bordón mano ternura," el bordón es la cuerda del arpa, que hace que suene como un bajo, es fuerte lo que le da esa textura a la canción. ¿Qué más? Bueno lo demás es algo que sí es entendible; un "ventarrón" es como un viento con lluvia. Y cuando habla de "teje el joropo bandoleras amarguras" es como que.. "bandoleras" se refiere a la bandola que es el instrumento que yo toco, como algo que enlaza la bandola con el espíritu y la vaina.. Es medio complicao que me entiendas pero bueno más o menos por ahí!

A flor de piel

The impropriety of death
never arose as a wax doll she wasn't.

Instead the fistful of person
expired like Merlin into a felt pouch
that Mamá called pretty and medieval
when she sent me a photo on WhatsApp.

Seeds graze the inside of the maraca
pulling a dust with no pearlescence
never to be held
in the palm to glisten
never to be prized in the sun.

Pulsera

Póntela pues
es tuya.

Nilometer

A nilometer is a graduated pillar or other vertical surface indicating the height reached by the Nile during its annual floods.

Now it indicates the different levels reached by the Orinoco
as expressed
in granite color
gradations.

These are the mundanities of our PETRODRAMA.

Obrero y Estudiante

Tío y Padre

En el taller
se come Chis Tris
se toma Chinotto
y me cuenta la otra Gladys
cómo fue que entraron una vez
a robarlos.

Rey más mago
menos nacimiento
¿Y ahora qué hago?

En Chichiriviche
arañita montada sobre mi pecho
Gladys se porta mal, cuenta sus billetes rosados
me pega con la mano,
¡'Chacha! Tenías un bicho.

Si el azabache obliga

Azabache
a form of coal carved
into the shape of a fist fastened
to a gold bracelet given
to newborns to ward off
cómo se dice
"evil eye."

                A que a tu gentileza sirva la higa

                Mi mano contra el mal de ojo

"jet" from Andalusian Arabic "sabaj"
    meaning obsidian
from Middle Persian "sab"
    meaning night.

Hora de remedios

When I wouldn't drink it she said *Fine!*
More liquid Motrin for me
more Vicks for me
more Merthiolate for me.

The palm is solar, simple, and seated.

The egg in the water is the infant
protected by intention and leavened power
and the migration of geological practice
is cracked over a bed of boiled cornmeal masa.

Deep Fake Deep

The only Earth I have is Google.

The only place to bow is the bathroom floor
its tile lightly splashed with dried
Barbie-pink nail polish from that one time.

Mamá sends photos of Gladys
now in a wheelchair somehow farther than before
her serene expression
in a floral dress among thin flowers
a child now after all that meanness

and in all her former meanness I want
to shield her from "having been mean."

I try to fall asleep and there is her face
placid in the WhatsApp photo
the flowers grow thinner
I strain through
the moment of thinning.

Norwegian YouTubers post GoPro videos
of their epic Roraima hikes.

Somewhere in Key Biscayne at my grandparents' feet
I play with their quaint pink cash like it's Monopoly money.

We have "World Heritage Day"
and Mamá sends me to school in a típico dress
I twirl on the concrete yard for my classmates to see
the red and yellow and white blur.
Mamá says ¡*Típico!*
at the dust stains
from the playground slide.

APOTROPAIA: Ancient Port
now filled with sand

The sun comes up on anywhere, pulls up on anyone
digging in the dirt.

Divide the jet amongst the elders, give a tiny piece to the child.

There was a storm that flung ancient pirates away and heaped them
on the shores of Lycia where they found all the bracelets.

A mid-Atlantic ridge
tumbling over
like Romans falling
on their hands.

The gazing continent wants to bundle up the newborn
and avert the gaze

and the nautical pentameter,
the pentatonic illusions
submerged and polyvocal.

Horus remedy

Líbrame del agua, ojéalo
baño de oro en vez de
oro pelao.

What's preserved in the vision
when your molecular threads are entwined
your metamorphic selves battled, spun a terrible dance
and landed in you; your cellular self runs ahead
of your transient self your feudal complicit self.

You swim or stay
you're in the bog now you're in the valley
you won't swim so Papá says you must
at the Doral public pool, he's like *It's time, everybody has their time.*

A haze;
                tus seres queridos que de repente no se querían
                What's an amulet for in a hall of mirrors?
                What's a talisman for in a tomb?

Inside the pool and the mad-mute world
you plug your nose and spin around to watch the light threading
the meniscus.

deep
sleep

*Sabana sin sol ni luna
¿Quién es el que bebe arena
en la noche más oscura?*

En la noche más oscura

Vine turns into bark and the city
I keep seeing in my sleep
does not exist
a woody paper climbs up, overtaking the pale green sinews.

I have been going to places that don't exist
since at least the fifth
grade and writing it down.

Mamá says it's normal and she does it all the time
it's called Astral Projection
and I then go
read about it on the floor
between the New Age and Spirituality shelves at Borders.

Mamá waters the blood red
poinciana, whispers to it: *You're beautiful*
and says she's also predicted the future
by going to the site of her prediction
right before waking up.
I believe her.

I type this all into Yahoo and go to my room
and stare at the wall
where the sea grape outside
casts golden solar clusters.

Light comes in and passes
through the crosshatch of all the things we make
but we're done making things and ready
to join the light
remembering as we do
through our vanished gills
that dark day when we pierced the surface.

I am happy to report
I have found the best place
for the mums
I've left them on the dining room table
and gone to meet my friends.

Took the Metrorail to Government Center
when I'm back the light will be thrown
on the dining room wall.

Sunlight burns the surface of the table
reluctant astonished bipeds up from our knuckles
not anywhere near a garden
scratched on a lignite wall.

The daughter

My mother has been visited by birds all her life
they alight on her balcony like she's Sleeping Beauty.

Franco Zeffirelli's La Traviata was a tolling bell
in our house
she would cry a lot about it
this opera beginning and ending
with bloody coughs.

¿Qué tiene? I would ask

La verdad es que no sé,
ni ella sabe,
escúchale la voz.

When she was angry with me my mother would say I was "just like my grandmother." Hearing this I imagined that brassy head in a foam neck brace, una MALA.

I said to her *I am not your mother you are*
my mother
I am myself telling you

I learned English with you.

In the end every time Alfredo is too late
Violeta dissolves into Elizabethan linens
and sends a mournful wave of pigeons into the Paris dawn.

My mother's eyes shine in the refrigerated light of the Panasonic.
Manola, Papá says emerging from the lazurite hallway
¿Cuándo se acaba esta vaina?

En Cumanacoa

Resulta que el papá de abuela Conchita era el 'todero' de su pueblo (el que hace todo); una persona que es capaz de hacer cualquier cosa.

Bueno eniwei; el papá de tu abuela Conchita era telegrafista también. Todero, pues: hacía de todo. Así cuenta tu tía Mercedes:

Próspero Flores, el todero. Si iba a parir una yegua, lo llamaban, si iba a parir una mujer, lo llamaban. Él era el boticario; ¿cómo se dice? Un apothecary, farmacista, con remedios naturales. Él reparaba las vainas rotas en el pueblo.

Un día, a una persona en el pueblo se le gangrenó una mano, por infección, pienso. Llamaron a Próspero y vio que se le tenía que cortar la mano, no quedaba otra.

Le cortan la mano al tipo, y la mandan a enterrar en el patio. ¡ENTIERRA ESA MANO! Alguien enterró la mano, se acabó y se dejó esa mano en el patio.

Al otro día están comiendo en la mesa y de repente ven que pasa por el comedor una de las gallinas.. con la mano en el pico, ¡toda hincha'!

Tu abuela salió corriendo, pegando gritos, la pobre. Estos son los Flores, mi familia.

Dormilona

Girls pacing in nightgowns
long sleeve or sleeveless
lace trim
cotton Swiss dot
hand-embroidered flowers across the bodice
from Upton's or ROSS.

Light subtle ruffling
pre-shrunk Victorian-style gown
floral smocking
breathable.

In a store window in Soho
a woman holds her face in front of a mirror
and pulls her skin back with her hands.

I see this and go home
and do the same.

This is the costume for my transit
to the other side.

Duérmase mi niña que tengo que hacer
lavar los pañales ponerme a coser.

Duérmase mi niña que tengo que hacer
lavar los pañales, ponerme a coser.

In Miami I twisted the fabric over la batea to wring out the watery Ariel detergent
before hanging the garment in the laundry room.

Reconsidering, I took it out to the yard
and laid it on the outstretched branches of the night.

¡El edificio se está cayendo!
¡Mamá, bendición!

Me despierto del susto.

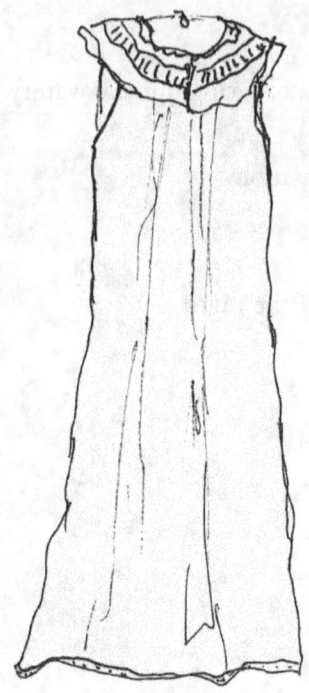

Dormilona para salir a regar a las matas

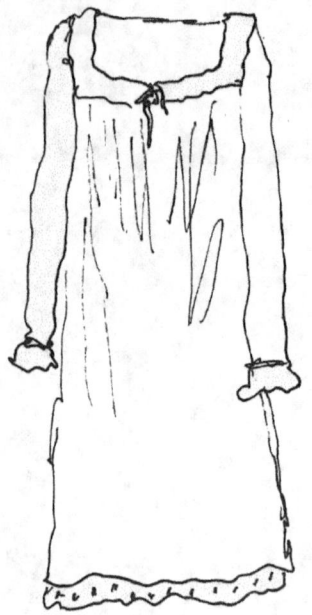

Dormilona para salir a mirar la luna

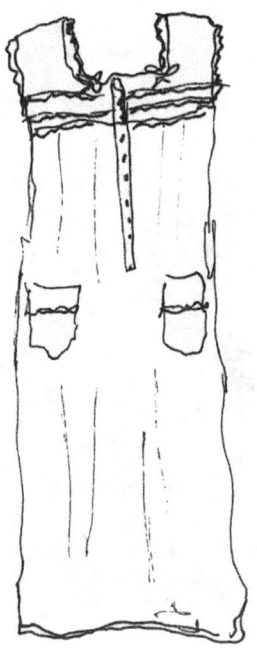

Dormilona para los sueños lúcidos

sleep data

*Duele lo que se perdió
cuando no se ha defendío.*

Cuando no se ha defendío

The brain is & is not
rewarded.

The less that is left
to my imagination
the more that is left
to my imagination.

When you found me in the ocean
holding a glass above water
you filled it
thank you.

When you waded back to shore
violent waves took me over
and all the fluid became the same.

Here comes the night.

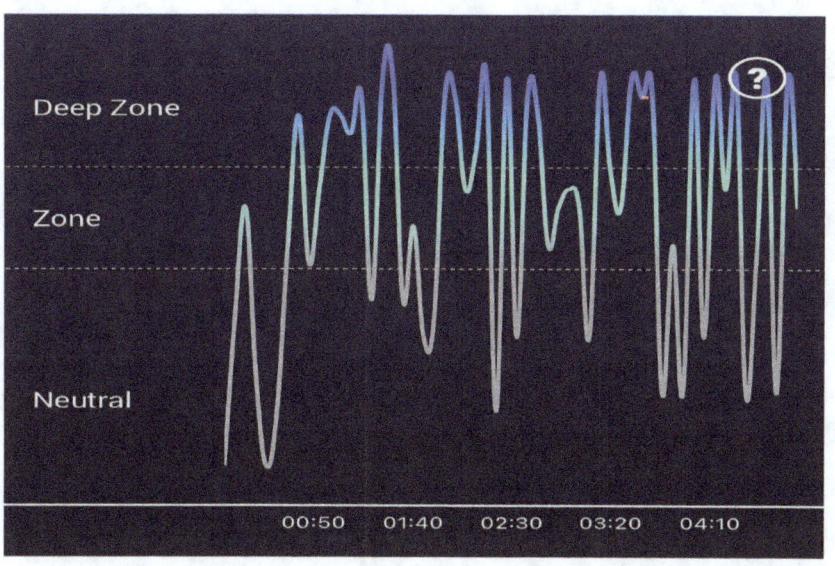

Dieu réunit ceux qui s'aiment

Her mother saved her daughter my mother   and her cousins my cousins

                        daughter my mother
from drowning in

                a whirlpool
                                      in the Caribbean Sea

by extending one of her son's

      my mother's brother's   my uncle's crutches

                                    her son's my mother's
brother's   mother saved

      her daughter

by pulling the children out   one by one.

Mandan a decir

Que Gladys se cayó
y está malita, en cama,
ahora recuerda hasta menos que antes
y a la vez, traviesa que es
recuerda de repente
todo.

Finally the doctor says
Párkinson's in
the WhatsApp audio.

El ojo

Lead me out of the forest
circling until the abrupt edge
holds us in for long
enough to find a rivulet down.

The eternal internal trees
spring up in a zapped region
breaking apart the night's eye
I surrender to a mesh of lightning
over Lake Maracaibo.

Your First Neurofeedback Session

Clouds gather above the hedges
they are smoke.

Lights come on in the darkened city
the darkest at midday.

The county beats
the fire back
the sky descends
to meet it.

Mandan mensajes sobre la abuela:
la señora
tiene déficit neurológico
      está muy bien cuidada, pero hay algunas cosas.

Amor Eterno

*Claro, quiero dedicar esta canción con mucho amor y respeto
más que una canción es una oración de amor que quiero dedicar
como siempre
y con el mismo amor, cariño y respeto
a todas las mamás que esta noche me han venido a visitar.
Sobre todo, para aquellas que están un poquito más lejos de mi.*

The rainforest is older than thinking, and I think my way back to it. The melaleuca bark peels off, extinct fruits exist again, major poles and portals reopen and close. Ambivalent underwater volcanoes arrange their porous islands. Plateaus above the canopy bear exposed amethyst fields. Long-armed frogs attach themselves to crystal trees, clouds brush the burning ponds. Nobody knows what happens in the sky.

The word for "heaven" and "sky" is the same in many languages. Since we make a distinction in English, heaven is further occluded and extinguished from the realm of matter. In the morning we wake up and say *Good morning mi cielo*. Blue fills the room.

Soñar despierta

Mamá sends videos on WhatsApp, Gladys is confined to a bed or a wheelchair and one can't distinguish her arms from the armrests.

In airports all over the country, I looked out the tall windows to see the earth. We had no language to tell each other we were lonely.

!Di McDonald's! my cousins would ask, *Say it in your American voice!* and like a nickelodeon I'd say it for them each time they requested, *McDonald's*, and they would laugh, amazed, how could I sound like that? How did I do that? What's lonelier than not knowing how I did that?

Making a life

The pink ocean recedes until there are only cold salted sidewalks.

There is an infinity of things that I do not know. Gladys has been dead for a long time, whatever a long time is. I counted on her as the one who would venture in my stead. It cannot be easy to be the skeptic, the one who answers meanness with reciprocal meanness, or the one who holds the pain of neglect.

I loved "connect the dots" as a child. I liked not knowing what the suspended mass of numbered dots would turn out to be and the gradual surprise. When my parents reminded me *We didn't come here for you to be a poet* they might have also meant they didn't come here for me to enjoy not knowing things.

I would have been a poet if we stayed in Venezuela, and they would have had words with me there as well. They might have said instead *Your cousin is an engineer.* And Gladys would have advised me that she also writes poems but doesn't go making a life out of them. Even though she did make a life out of them, I saw her.

Women have been asked to send their time out like a cord for others to grasp and guide. Gladys curled away from death until she coiled right in, like a fly into a bromeliad. She berated the neighbor's child, she refused to eat, and she didn't believe what anyone said to her. The neighbors and the doctors enclosed her with tender concern, but it was obvious from any distance that the horizon was winding up to meet the moon.

The forest ensnares us because our brain is already its coarse diorama. This is why we get lost in forests, why they can cloister us without a static barrier, and why we are crestfallen by the first red leaf that floats down from a powdery elm in Central Park. Carl Sagan said we are the cousins of trees, and in her essay, "Tree Time," Sumana Roy describes how fleeting, how incidental humans are to trees. We are their shadows. Men have launched into the forest for ages to pierce their sides for us.

Enrique said I could roll down every window in the LTD Crown Vic if I wanted, I could press all the silly car buttons and wear his cowboy hat. What a delight; to be a little girl with a grandfather who laughed at everything, collected rainwater with us, and gave out one hundred Bolívares when asked only for fifty. It was a good thing that he had me to scramble the radio dial, that he had my mother to laugh at his Spanglish puns, that he had the entire neighborhood to hold his gentle, transcendent countenance in their shining eyes.

Mamá holds Gladys' poems on her lap, now. She sifts and reads them, and I have a difficult time concentrating. The notebook sheets and invoices are thin and soft, like the white curls that sat on Gladys' head above the hard frown line. Their envelope rests on my mother's legs, a halo of paper fuzz, and she plies the scrap poems carefully like she's passing her hand through her mother's hair; like she never could in real life, like she is a little sorry she could have tried more. Then I am sorry too like I could have seen my mother better, like my mother could have seen hers better, like the periscope was so foggy, who took our eyes?

Miss Universo

Not to worry
we'll fix you.

I was the same
but we'll make you different.

See how she's walking
better than the others

see how she answers
better?

You weren't supposed to be like this
balancing on the bike seat
showing off to the boys
winning their marbles.

The consultation goes fine
they simulate before and after photos.

Driving home from the clinic
there's traffic on the Palmetto and looking out
at the airport runway
I say I'd rather live a life in which I never cut my face.

Sleep study

Willing the body to pursue the forest dream is a study. The neuroscience majors from Stanford eat gummy bears with me at the function and offer to loan me a machine. It falls through.

It falls through. Mamá sends a digital transfer of a cassette tape recording of Gladys telling me all about when I will visit her and update her on the things I have learned, including how to read. Wiping the calathea leaves I whisper *You're beautiful*.

Wiping the calathea leaves I whisper *You're beautiful*. What if I simply "invent" the sleep study, its parameters and metrics, and its transfer of unconscious imprints, like the time I reverse-processed some old color slides I found in an abandoned building? The sleep study data can be imperfect like the recollection of a dream, which is imperfect memory processing imperfect processing.

The sleep study data can be imperfect like the recollection of a dream, which is imperfect memory processing imperfect processing. Taking up sketching nightgowns again, I invite Gladys' cassette tape voice to accompany me, and she says things like *Keep going. It's just for practice.*

It's just for practice. The University of Texas at Masaguaral Biological Station conducts the longest study of parrotlets in Venezuela and focuses specifically on vocal imitation. Ornithologists determined in 2007 that "contact calls" were used by the parrotlets to identify one another.

Ornithologists determined in 2007 that "contact calls" were used by the parrotlets to identify one another. Mamá says her phone, near-rupture like an overheated Pillsbury tube, is too full of data to receive videos or voice notes. Like a parakeet alighting from one branch to another, she migrates between apps to retrieve my parceled messages.

Like a parakeet alighting from one branch to another, she migrates between apps to retrieve my parceled messages. I copy all of this and text it to her. Here, in Oakland, Spring announces itself in starlings murmuring over the schoolyard.

Challenger, January 1986

Event horizons are neither
beginning nor end.
The formula trailed into the folds
of my swaddling blanket
      because Mamá watched the news.
Something stopped time
as if I could understand language yet—
as if fluid time and fabric
had folded me onto a new coast.

She covered the top
of my head
and a starfish melted down from the square morning sky.
A new cone of time opens
when you pass into singularity and you mimic
                      MAMAMAMAMAMA
                        MU
                        UIM
                        MUUMUU
                        UIIUMIUUIMUIIUMIUUIMUIIU

There is as much folding space
as there never was—
Ay she spoke softly, aged twenty-six
chestnut hair fastened in a pink banana clip, *Dios mio*
No puede ser.
She drew me near in my unknowing

I struggle with time
because what is it
a mirror

                        time where I come from
                        if I come from
                        anywhere
                        it's this knowing

                                                infinite orbit.

Cantos de Sirenas

I woke up in the middle of the night, another dream about swimming. A chicken fight in the silt-tinted brackish sound between the shore and a wooded island. My tíos rented a small motorboat and we took turns crossing over. The wind lifted my curls and my cousin Enrique patted my head like I was a poodle.

The city of Valencia has a waterpark called Parque Dunas, where I used to go with my cousins to talk to the boys who ran the slides. They have tubing rides in chlorinated inlets throughout the park, painted palm tree fountains, and various other structures raining blue water on parkgoers.

My Brooklyn roommates invited me to the beach. We took the Q to Coney Island, scraps of Nathan's Famous tray paper encircled us in the air. Later, changing into a nightgown in my room, I saw a man in the window across the alley waving at me. I can still see his delirious silhouette ensconced in red brick.

When the Italians arrived they found that the communities of the coast lived in stilt homes, which is not uncommon in the Caribbean, and is particular to the Orinoco river basin. Like the ancient Chinampas in Mexico, there were complex waterways coursing between purposeful structures, and this inspired the Italians to name the region after their fave. Little Venice they said. In Iceland, while paying for fish & chips, the cashier asks where I am from. Mishearing, she says she's actually been to Minnesota and that it is very nice.

Yo Soy el Romero Santo
Yo Soy el Romero Santo
Y si no me necesitas
¿Para qué me nombras tanto?

I am my own mother
and my own child
I swim to the surface.

Oyeme San Juan Bautista te voy a pedir un favor
te voy a pedir un favor
Que me aclares la garganta
Para cantarte mejor.

When the earliest land dwellers broke water
they pierced the meniscus and split the body.
I swim to the surface, the drums chirrup
in the air.

En el espacio y sobre el dormido mar

My neurofeedback technician congratulates me over the phone on the "optimal" functioning of my brain. I've been scoring points in the "deep zone" over the last two weeks. Someone on TikTok says a path to healing is to nurture the child within, to find them and give them love, if even retroactively. But then I think what about the me of last April? Searching for potting soil at Home Depot? Neither mythologized nor time-brushed.

I think of my synapses like the shivering dial tone, the trill of sticks and hands, so many of these songs are about wanting to sing but not knowing how to. Sing as in signaling the sadness of a continent coursing through european instruments. En Cuba dicen que *antes de morir yo quiero cantar mis versos del alma.*

I think of my synapses like the shivering family tree; my ancestors teaching their children how to fish, writing poems in the sand and then bashfully brushing them back to oblivion with their hands— eyes burning.

Time of Death

Midway through
a lecture a
student mentions hearing
that we were in our maternal grandmother's
ecosystem   that is to say
grandmother produced mother
and mother's components   including
the ones that produced us so

There's a reason for all of these midnight lucidities these
ideating lights on I-95 reminding me of a past I never saw

"After You've Gone" comes on through an untuned upright piano
like a set of dentures sunk into a glass of water

i carry your heart(i carry it in my heart)

Gladys liked to lie on her Georgian sofas
and tell me terrible things as if by dictation as if
via seance

When I was five she recounted
her life and the pain of it I stood
before her like a hologram from the future
for the grief to pass through
particulate and unmoored

Well, anyway, she concluded, *let's practice dialing 911.*

We don't know the time
although the country once
unilaterally altered national time
and Gladys loved that.
Aló, Presidente! with its absurd din
on the Panasonic through the night
blankets her in a soft pallor cast upon her sighing
in her dormilona, glowing with a final
reprieve in something, anything, that she chose for herself.

Duérmase mi niña

Venetian blinds
pattern themselves on the wall
same as ever
canals of blue light.

Is it the moon like Gladys
saying *Aqui estoy*
saying *¡Tampoco te esperes!*

How did our 19th-century relatives
view the blue screens of their nearish tech?
Sliding a hand across
the daguerreotype, kind of knowing; *Por ahí vienen
cosas tremendas.* Peering into the future they felt
the arrogant light coming,
the coiled wire a gravitational lensing.

The blinds stamped on the wall
bring me closer to the linguistic abyss
we are from. The cruciferous brain intuits nothing in the forest.

Delta Delta Delta
We land in MIA and remember English
the letters fall on their sides and become threads
undulating then frozen on the wall.

I look up and see the acne-scarred moon
adolescent, not understanding,
paddling into the riptide.

Truman Sleeps

Near-death experience reporters say they "escaped time"
how did they know?

Christof watches from the fake moon
am I Christof watching me from the fake moon?

The sleep center doctor and I
have a video consultation
he describes the ring that I will wear
It reads everything he assures me.

The energy bill arrives
imagine that; the energy bill arriving
with a tiny lightning bolt on the header.

I guess right before falling asleep
is time.

Maybe you could have seen something beyond this,
says my mother, then you never would have coiled
from the center of the bed into your abyss of unknowing.

A sudden relief, rising from the graded stone
[[middle consciousness]]

The sleep center doctor
cannot tell me where I went
You went to your brain, he might say
You went to the forest.

"Kenneth Ring subdivided the NDE into a five-stage continuum using Moody's nine-step experiment as inspiration. The subdivisions were:

1. Peace
2. Body separation
3. Entering darkness
4. Seeing the light
5. Entering another realm of existence, through the light"

El campo

Allá lejos viene un barco
y en él viene mi amor
se viene peinando un crespo a pie del palo mayor.

The vessel used to be farther out
a speck
disconcerting but distant

it used to be like wind on the water
but now it taps the walls.

Allá lejos viene un barco
Allá lejos viene un barco

Waves pull the gathering family
placing objects on towels
they recede further.

La garza prisionera no canta cual solía—

¿Que hago yo,
sola en el campo?
¿Que hago yo en el campo sola?

Gladys Magdalena Flores
Nov. 6, 1933, Cumanacoa - Nov. 29, 2020, Valencia

Gladys, Manola y Conchita, Chichiriviche, 1959
(Photo courtesy of Francis Oliver)

Acknowledgments

I have attempted to throw away much of my writing throughout my life. My mother continually fished those documents out of the bin and assembled them in envelopes and folders, sometimes presenting them to me and saying, "You wrote this!" I am thankful to her for this tender gesture that emanates across time as the deeply human impulse to preserve one another.

This book began to take form in 2018, and there have been many contributors to the overall project in a variety of meaningful ways. I have consulted with musicians, textile workers, designers, and translators while developing this project. I am very thankful to the supportive community of poets, artists, readers, friends, and family who have thoughtfully and lovingly engaged with this work since I began composing it.

Thanks to A Velvet Giant, Columbia Journal, Ayin Press, Islandia Journal, and Denver Quarterly for featuring poems from this book over the years. Thank you to the various spaces and program coordinators who have collaborated with me on dormilona readings and projects. Thank you to Christina Drill for your eternal support and for curating a conversation about the poems.

Finally, thank you to Ryan Rivas at Burrow Press, Gloria Muñoz, Katie Jean Shinkle, and Urayoán Noel for your support and profoundly considerate engagement with this collection.

Manola, Caracas, 1965
(Photo courtesy of Francis Oliver)

References

- "The Lost Pilot" by James Tate is referenced in "El Piloto Perdido"
- "Florentino y El Diablo," a Venezuelan folk poem by Alberto Torrealba, is referenced at the opening of each section of this collection and mirrors the Porfía structure of Joropo music.
- The folk song "Polo Margariteño" is referenced across the collection
- The poem "i carry your heart with me(i carry it in]" by E.E. Cummings is referenced in "Time of Death"
- The poem "Amor Eterno" is a reference to the eponymous song by Juan Gabriel, and his dedication during a live concert is quoted in the poem.

Images

p. 20 – Family portrait, Caracas, 1965; original photograph torn by Gladys to remove her face

p. 61 – Various family photographs were taken between 1955 and 1965

p. 64 – Nightgown illustrations, ink on sketch paper

p. 69 – Mindlyft screenshot from Neurofeedback session

p. 75 – Juan Gabriel, image from YouTube video of concert

p. 86 – Enrique and Gladys' Wedding, Iglesia San Juan Bautista, 1955

About the Author

Connie Mae Oliver is a poet and artist living in the San Francisco Bay Area. Her first book of poems, *Cosmos A Personal Voyage by Carl Sagan Ann Druyan Steven Soter And Me* (Operating System, 2017) is about nuclear disarmament. Her second book, *Science Fiction Fiction* (Spuyten Duyvil, 2020) is an homage to Miami-Dade County and color photography in the early aughts.

www.ingramcontent.com/pod-product-compliance
Lightning Source LLC
Chambersburg PA
CBHW070156080526
44586CB00015B/2010